MW00436822

PROFESSIONAL DEVELOPMENT THAT STICKS

How do I create meaningful learning experiences for educators?

Fred
ENDE

ASCD Alexandria, VA USA

Website: www.ascd.org
E-mail: books@ascd.org

ASCD | arias™
www.ascdarias.org

Printed in the United States of America. ASCD publications present a variety of viewpoints. The views expressed or implied in this book should not be interpreted as official positions of the Association.

ASCD®, ASCD LEARN TEACH LEAD®, ASCD ARIAS™, and ANSWERS YOU KNOW FROM VOICES YOU TRUST® are trademarks owned by ASCD and may not be used without permission. All other referenced trademarks are the property of their respective owners.

PAPERBACK ISBN: 978-1-4166-2193-5   ASCD product #SF116040

Also available as an e-book (see Books in Print for the ISBNs).

Library of Congress Cataloging-in-Publication Data

Names: Ende, Fred, author.
Title: Professional development that sticks : how do I create meaningful learning experiences for educators? / Fred Ende.
Description: Alexandria, Virginia : ASCD, [2016] | Includes bibliographical references.
Identifiers: LCCN 2015049291 (print) | LCCN 2015051326 (ebook) | ISBN 9781416621935 (pbk.) | ISBN 9781416621959 (PDF)
Subjects: LCSH: Teachers--In-service training.
Classification: LCC LB1731 .E535 2016 (print) | LCC LB1731 (ebook) | DDC 370.71/1--dc23
LC record available at http://lccn.loc.gov/2015049291

23 22 21 20 19 18 17 16   1 2 3 4 5 6 7 8 9 10

PROFESSIONAL DEVELOPMENT THAT STICKS

How do I create meaningful learning experiences for educators?

Sticky Questions 1

PDL Phase I: Planning 13

PDL Phase II: Providing 30

PDL Phase III: Following Up.. 40

Acknowledgments.. 48

Encore 51

References 57

About the Author... 58

Want to earn a free ASCD Arias e-book?
Your opinion counts! Please take 2–3 minutes to give
us your feedback on this publication. All survey
respondents will be entered into a drawing to
win an ASCD Arias e-book.

Please visit
www.ascd.org/ariasfeedback

Thank you!

Sticky Questions

It's Tuesday afternoon at 3:30. It's been an amazing day teaching science to your 8th grade students. Great work has taken place, and you have a million and one things to do in order to get ready for tomorrow. However, there's a faculty meeting (which would be fine, except for the fact that according to the agenda, it looks like a "sit 'n git" session led by an expert speaking on a topic with little relation to middle school, let alone middle school science), and you're feeling pretty mindwiped at the end of the day. But you know you have to go, so you give up what you want to do and attend. As you sit there trying to absorb the information being shared, you ask yourself the often present question, "Why am I here?"

Sound familiar? This dismal picture is all too often what professional development (or PD) looks like: generic, impersonal, and largely forgettable. Why has this become the norm for educators? Why isn't their PD more engaging, relevant, and impactful? The sad truth is that there is a lack of agreement in the field about what "good PD" is and what it looks like, leaving many leaders with only a vague idea of how to provide their teachers with PD that will stick and have a lasting positive effect on both teachers and students. To demonstrate this point, let's begin with a quick quiz. I'll ask the questions, and you supply the answers. Easy, right? Here we go.

1. Professional development is . . .

    A. An opportunity to grow as a professional.
    B. A boring, wasteful chore.
    C. Something over which I have no control.
    D. All of the above.
    E. None of the above.

2. Professional development and personal learning are similar/different *(circle one)* because

    _____.

3. In order for professional development to stick or be long-lasting, I need to make sure I do the following:

    _____.

4. Which of the following five activities are examples of professional development? Why?

    A Attending an Edcamp conference event to serve as a session facilitator.
    B. Attending an Edcamp conference event as a participant.
    C. Reading the *Marshall Memo*.
    D. Meeting to discuss professional development needs with the district superintendent and assistant superintendent for curriculum.
    E. Engaging in face-to-face and virtual conversations with colleagues about the meaning of the word *perception* and how it affects our lives as educators and parents.

After responding to these four questions, I have no doubt you had trouble settling on one answer for each. This is probably a quiz you'd want to avoid if you had to select one "correct" response.

That's the funny thing about professional development. There isn't really a "right" answer in terms of what it is, how it works, or when it should happen. There are a lot of supporting ideas, sure, and we often do a decent job of explaining what it *shouldn't* be, how it *can't* work, or when it *shouldn't* happen. But none of that really gets to the heart of why professional development is so important and why it has to stick when we engage in it. We'll come back to the idea of "stickiness" throughout this book; first, let's define what professional development really is.

What Is Professional Development?

Like the duck-billed platypus, professional development is often easy to spot but difficult to categorize. We know it when we experience it and can see it happening, but we don't always know what it's all about. The purpose of professional development is pretty easy to speak to. In my ten years as a science teacher and department chair—and five additional combined years as a curriculum program director and assistant director of curriculum—I have yet to find the leader or learner who disagrees with this statement:

> All of us, no matter what role we hold, no matter what organization we work for, no matter what profession we belong to, need to strive to keep getting better. And getting better requires lots of work—work that we often don't yet know how to do on our own.

Even though professional development has existed in American education since the days of the "common school" (in some form or another), it wasn't until the second half of the 20th century that school populations began to grow racially, ethnically, and developmentally diverse, requiring teachers to think and teach differently in order to truly help all learners succeed. Early professional development was of the "sit 'n git" variety, which usually involved teachers attending assigned sessions for a designated number of hours. During these sessions, teachers might have taken notes, asked questions, or simply done their best to keep up with the pace of the information provided.

Was this effective? By today's standards, no. Nevertheless, this traditional form of professional development matched the nature of the teaching and learning that was going on in classrooms at the time. This doesn't mean that it was any more or less effective, but it does mean that the professional development experienced by educators was often similar to how teachers were learning with and leading their own students. With the passage of the Elementary and Secondary Education Act (ESEA) in 1965, an increase in federal funds began to help the neediest students become more successful. This also meant there were additional opportunities to structure professional development for teachers. The findings of the Coleman Report in 1966 helped put an emphasis on the power of PD by showcasing that a variety of factors (e.g., teacher preparation, stakeholder communication ability, learner sense of control) truly created a comprehensive learning environment (Kaestle, 2001).

As the 1970s began, more and more teachers engaged in professional development. Unfortunately, though, much of this professional development was conducted in a way that didn't stick—it didn't have a positive long-term impact on teaching and learning. The 1970s might be a decade that's remembered for a number of things, but by all accounts, professional development isn't one of them.

Almost 50 years later, professional development has generally remained the same. A good portion of PD still consists largely of "you sit, I talk" or "one size fits all" sessions. Often, those who are ostensibly being developed have little or no say in the development itself, and leaders sometimes consider PD as an afterthought—something that must be done but for which there isn't a ton of available time.

Well, there goes your good mood, huh? Fear not; it isn't all doom and gloom. Professional development can indeed be lasting and incredibly sticky, and it can make a tremendous difference for educators. Even the most traditional forms of PD can have a powerful effect, if matched with the right audience, provided at an appropriate time, and delivered in an effective way. Consider, for instance, how teachers might react to two hours of lecture-based professional development held before school and led by an incredibly engaging facilitator versus two hours of lecture-based professional development held after school and led by a dull presenter. I've been a participant in both scenarios, and I can tell you clearly: one was much stickier for me than the other.

The purpose of this book, then, is to provide you with a number of ideas and practical strategies to design, implement, and reflect on PD that truly sticks. And as you'll see, it doesn't have to be as hard as we might think it is, especially given the preponderance of PD that seems to lack purpose. Before we go in depth about planning, providing, and following up on powerful PD, though, we have two more stops to make.

PD? PL? How about PDL?

As an avid user of social media, I see posts every day that are full of complaints about professional development and focus on debates, questions, and clarifications about how it compares to personalized learning. Over time, I've realized that professional development and personalized learning are really two sides of the same learning coin. Here's why:

- Research finds that the best professional development is focused on the learner as an individual, is engaging, requires follow up, and has direct applicability to the audience's role (Guskey, 2009).
- According to the International Society for Technology in Education, personalized education experiences focus on the learner, are engaging and allow for deep learning, require regular follow up, and are tied to a learner's given role (Basye, 2014).

As you can see, both concepts actually can—and should—go hand in hand. In fact, the most accurate reference isn't PD or PL; rather, it's PDL, because **P**rofessional **D**evelopment for **L**earning is what it really needs to be about. Without a focus on instilling deep and sticky learning, PD won't mean a thing, and you can't have personal learning without some way to develop further as a professional. Therefore, the debate about whether we want to call it *professional development* or *personalized learning* is a nonstarter because when done well, both are inherently the same thing.

Professional development for learning should be meaningful for the deliverer, the audience, and those learners who are the end recipients of the learning (usually our students but could also be teachers, leaders, or parents). In fact, the best PDL is designed to have just as much impact on the facilitator of the learning as it does on students.

A tall order? Possibly, but research shows that continuing on our current path would be a bad idea. According to a Gallup poll conducted in the fall of 2014, superintendents throughout the United States—when asked about professional development—were able to cite a tremendous number of areas that were being explored with their staff (Gallup, Inc., 2014). It was clear that professional development was taking place, yet the data also illustrated the necessity and urgency of building professional capacity for PDL. Only one-third of those polled indicated that their districts had sufficient professional learning plans in place for new teachers, only a quarter of teachers (and half of principals) played an active role in determining PDL priorities, and only one-fifth of all districts supplied appropriate time for educator learning.

This begs the question: If we aren't providing our leaders and learners with the time and choice to cultivate their own learning, how can we in all fairness have high expectations of them? It's a sobering question. Thankfully, it's also one for which we can provide a positive answer. We just need to make some accessible changes to the way we structure our professional learning.

Making PDL Sticky

We can thank Malcolm Gladwell, author of the best-selling *The Tipping Point* (2000), for providing us with a way of looking at stickiness that moves beyond the gum on your shoe. Gladwell describes the key to what makes an initiative successful as its "stickiness factor" or how entwined it becomes in your whole way of being. In determining stickiness, he writes, "Is the message (or the food, or movie, or product) memorable? Is it so memorable, in fact, that it can create change, that it can spur someone to action?" (Gladwell, 2000, p. 92)

Gladwell has it right. Professional development for learning will have a more lasting impression if it remains in the minds of its target audience and causes them to take action. But what does this kind of PDL look like? Let's start with what we know. An excellent review of professional development needs was recently conducted by the Teacher Development Trust (2015) out of the UK. Based on their report, Guskey's analysis (2009), and my own experience as an assistant director of curriculum, we can reasonably determine that PDL works when

- It is meaningful to all three parts of the process (i.e., facilitator, audience, and learners down the line).

- It is highly engaging for the audience through hands-on activities and alignment to specific needs.
- The audience has a say in the PD being offered, and the learners at the end of the chain have an opportunity to reflect on the big picture.
- Enough time is provided for the facilitator to showcase the importance of the work, for the audience to sense its urgency, and for learners to see a difference in their learning experience.

Exploring each of these areas in depth is beyond the scope of this book, but we can examine the overarching effect of having them all together: stickiness. Now that we've pinpointed the four ingredients for making PDL sticky, we have to identify how to make this stickiness a reality.

That's where the Think, Act, Review (TAR) method comes in. Just like the end result it leads to, the TAR method is itself a sticky process. It has a memorable name, is easy and effective to use, and generates a strong feedback loop that makes you want to use it again and again. The TAR method guides my thinking as I plan, provide, and evaluate professional development for learning. Truly, it plays a tremendous role in the work that I do.

Professional development for learning consists of three phases. You start with the planning phase, where you consider all of the facets of what you hope to work on. Then you move on to the providing (or facilitating) phase, where you or your provider engages in the PDL with your audience. Finally, you finish with the following-up (or reflecting) phase. Great professional development doesn't end after it has been provided. The TAR method provides a framework for engaging in each of these phases to ensure a PDL experience that is both meaningful and long-lasting. (See Figure 1 for an outline of this framework and some key questions to guide you through each phase.)

- The *T* is all about *thinking*. Regardless of whether you're in the planning, providing, or following-up phase, careful study and deep thinking must be part of every step. For example, in the planning stage, you'll have to think about the purpose of your PDL, a structure that matches that purpose, and practical questions and logistics that will guide its development. When providing the PDL, you'll have to think about logistics and relationships. Not all PDL is created to be the same, and PDL that doesn't match its audience is bound to make it less effective. People, by nature, want to feel like they belong and have a say. When you're providing the PDL, you'll have to think about your facilitation and how attendees are engaging in the learning (or not). Of course, the following-up stage is also the time to think about all that juicy data sitting on your desk waiting to be analyzed.
- The *A*? That stands for *act*. As professional development leaders, we must serve in an acting role during all three phases. Even if you aren't personally the one providing the PD, you need to act on a number of key items to ensure each of the phases is successful. For example, as we'll discuss later, when I engage in the

FIGURE 1: **Questions to Guide Your PDL Design**

Phase	TAR Step	Key Guiding Questions
Planning	Think	• How do I determine a PDL purpose to guide my planning? • How will I go about collecting the data I need to plan?
	Act	• What steps do I take to engage in planning? • Who plays a role? Why? • What format best fits my PDL? • What logistics do I have to pay attention to?
	Review	• How do I make sure I've taken all of the details into consideration as I finalize plans? • Was I able to marry form and function to give this design what I believe will be a lasting impact? Why or why not? • Are there any last-minute adjustments I can make before the PDL begins to achieve a better fit? • Did I involve the right players? How do I know?
Providing	Think	• How can I use what I know about my learning space and the participants in my session to plan for adaptability? • How can I put relationship-building at the forefront of providing PDL?
	Act	• What implementation steps should I take when facilitating (or leading the facilitation of) PDL? • How can I be both a leader and a learner when providing PDL?
	Review	• In what ways can I reflect during the process of providing so I can make course corrections as the providing stage continues? • What data should I be collecting as I provide PDL?

FIGURE 1: **Questions to Guide Your PDL Design**
(*continued*)

Phase	TAR Step	Key Guiding Questions
Following Up	Think	• How can I use collected data from the providing phase to come up with ideas for change?
	Act	• In what ways can I use collected data to help facilitators (and myself) improve practice? • How do I provide constructive feedback that fosters growth? • How can I follow through with post-session follow-up?
	Review	• How do I use my work in this phase to serve as a springboard toward putting new PDL into action?

acting stage, I'm engaging in conversations with PDL providers to build a contract, leading the professional learning myself, learning alongside participants, or reading through PDL evaluations and putting together an analysis.

• Finally, the *R* represents careful *review*. All three phases require reflection to take place, and everyone involved in the process needs to be engaged in a continuous cycle of reflection. Reflecting and review can never be saved for the end. When planning, I constantly ask questions about whether the logistics will work as designed, and I regularly ask for input from colleagues to see what they think about a planned design. When providing PDL, I'm listening to conversations and asking myself questions about what participants are (and are not) learning. I'm also reflecting with providers, both during PDL sessions (e.g., during a break or lunch) and after (e.g., while recapping the event or discussing the session data analysis). When a session is complete, I also reflect on what to do next and what the future might hold for this type of work, this type of learning session, and this facilitator. It is important to remember that when you're reflecting, you're considering the perspectives of stakeholders at all levels, from students to district leaders.

Let's now turn our attention to PDL design and take a closer look at how we can apply the TAR method to each of the three PDL phases: planning, providing, and following up. You'll see, step by step, how this method puts us on a path toward professional development experiences that have a long-term positive impact on educators and all learners down the line.

PDL Phase I: Planning

"If you fail to plan, you are planning to fail."
—Benjamin Franklin

Benjamin Franklin might not have been talking about professional development in education when he coined that quote, but he certainly could have been. As a renowned tinkerer, philosopher, statesman, inventor, and theorist—to name just a few of his accomplishments—Franklin likely learned from his own experiences that the only way to stay on top of multiple shifting demands and responsibilities is to plan.

As we embark on the first phase of PDL, let's consider the following questions for reflection:

Think: How do I determine a PDL purpose to guide my planning?

Act: What steps do I take to engage in planning? Who plays a role? Why?

Review: How do I make sure I've taken all of the details into consideration as I finalize my plans?

Planning for PDL couldn't be more important, yet Guskey (2014) states that, regardless of what history (and various educational groups) say about its effectiveness, "One thing on which all groups agree is that professional learning, whether individual or in groups, is rarely well planned" (p. 12).

We've all experienced professional learning sessions that appear out of place, and we've all sat through sessions where it was difficult to make connections between the subject matter and where we were in our lives and careers. Why were we even involved in the first place? Examples such as these are far too common. Less common are the success stories. Perhaps some of us have been fortunate enough to engage in PDL that hits us at our core and is truly life-changing. What makes them successful? In most cases, it comes down to purpose and planning.

Think: Determine Purpose

All professional development needs purpose, but more importantly, that purpose must be less about the planner and more about the attendees. Too often, PD is designed in a vacuum. Those designing it think that it's right for a given audience, but they don't actually bother to get input to inform their decisions. To ensure that your PDL is meaningful, make the audience's perspective and preference the most influential factors in determining your purpose and goals. Ideally, the audience should dictate the purpose, but this may not always be possible. For example, the school may be embarking on a totally new endeavor, or the school or district may be inflexible. In situations such as these, it is best that the purpose influences who is selected for that PDL session and that it doesn't become an initiative trying to cater to everyone.

In the best-case scenario, your planning should be based on feedback you have received from previous PDL sessions. If you don't have previous experience to draw from, you'll be starting from scratch. If this is the case, then you might want to let a PDL initiative take a back-seat to active listening and culture learning. This will help you determine what type of feedback will best inform your work going forward. Either way, feedback can be collected in a variety of ways. Some of the most effective ways of collecting feedback are personal conversations about what people would like to work on (which works best with smaller audiences) or short surveys of no more than five or six questions (which can be placed in staff mailboxes or emailed using a free online tool). What types of questions should be asked? Consider the following examples:

- What areas would be most beneficial for you to work on during the upcoming year? Why?
- What are areas that you would prefer not to work on during the upcoming year? Why?
- What are areas in which your students could use additional support? Why?
- What will your learning look like over the course of this year? How do you envision it?
- Think ahead to next year. What do you hope to have learned by then?

Consider the mode of data collection you plan to use. Will you collect data via an online survey, a written document, or something else entirely? Choose a form, put it to use, and then make sure that you survey attendees after the learning session has ended. (See Figure 2 for an example.) Online surveys are a great way to collect simple qualitative and quantitative data. The majority of free data-collection tools will also do some basic analysis of your data. A challenge with online surveys is the low response rate. When I use them, I'm lucky if I get more than a 20–25 percent response rate. It's not that participants are actively choosing not to respond, but often, once we've left a session, we get caught back up in the stream of information overload that fills our workdays. An email requesting your response to a past PDL session? That's not necessarily at the top of everyone's priority list.

Written responses gathered at the end of a learning session or leading into a break are a great way to get detailed qualitative data. Participants tend to be more comfortable writing more when others are doing the same thing, and nothing beats collecting data when the information is still fresh in attendees' minds. I've found that if I distribute evaluations with roughly 15 minutes left in a PDL session and give enough time for participants to truly think about their responses, I get close to a 100 percent return rate.

What other data collection options do you have? One great way to collect incredibly detailed data is to select a subset of attendees and interview them. Sit down with them for a bit and chat, keeping track of targeted questions that you feel you need to ask. In selecting interviewees, you'll want to choose attendees whom you know are very different from one another—in other words, those who participate in PDL differently. By gathering data that cover a wide range of response types, you can maximize the usefulness of the results. We should never think of feedback opportunities as a chance to pat ourselves on the back. The key with planning for data collection is that we make it a priority and schedule the time to do it. Although some data are more helpful than others, the worst type of data is the type that wasn't collected.

FIGURE 2: **Sample Learning Session Evaluation Form**

Name of Participant:_____

Participating District:_____

Please check appropriate boxes:

Position: ☐ Teacher/TA   ☐ Administrator   ☐ Other

Level: ☐ Elementary   ☐ Middle   ☐ Secondary   ☐ District

- -

Thank you for attending this learning session. **We look forward to continuing to support your professional development. To help us provide you with even more effective educational experiences, we ask that you complete the questions that follow.**

Specifically, what ideas and/or materials from this session do you plan to use?

_____

_____

_____

What were the most valuable aspects of the session?

_____

_____

_____

What is one suggestion you would make to improve this session?

_____

_____

_____

What professional development opportunities would you like to see offered in the future?

_____

_____

_____

_____

What follow-up should be provided to make sure today's learning sticks for you?

_____

_____

_____

_____

How did you hear about this session, and why did you decide to attend it?

_____

_____

_____

_____

It's important to mention in your feedback mechanism that even though these questions are being asked of everyone, how you utilize the responses will depend on the full complement of data you receive. While you promise to give everyone a voice, you can't necessarily promise that each voice will lead to a PDL focus. What are areas in which your students could use additional support? Why? This question is a necessary one to ask because educators sometimes aren't sure what they themselves need, but when the question is framed in terms of what students need, they can usually respond better. After all, what students need most is often a reflection of where educators need to improve . . . whether we admit it to ourselves or not.

When planning for this year's catalog of PDL offerings, my director of curriculum and instruction and I held a "PD

Summit" with assistant superintendents and superintendents throughout the region. During the summit, we posed questions about the professional learning initiatives that were a focus for the current year and about what summit attendees projected to be hot topics for the following year. Attendees answered these questions on large sheets of poster paper and posted their responses on the walls. Then we conducted a gallery walk where everyone took a close look at each of the posters to see what their peers in other districts were working on. This not only helped my director and I learn what our districts needed for their respective PDL efforts but also helped districts recognize which of their colleagues they might reach out to for expertise and who they might contact to co-plan professional learning opportunities. For instance, a number of districts were considering exploring MakerSpace initiatives, which led us to design a number of regional workshops and also resulted in a support network for other districts who were heading down this path. By asking questions, allowing for reflection time, and making connections, we helped districts—and our curriculum department—determine purpose.

In situations where the school or district has already decided on the purpose for the PDL, it is important that only staff with relevant needs be selected to attend. Even so-called schoolwide or districtwide initiatives are rarely so general that PDL actually applies to everyone, and one of the worst moves we can make is to require all staff members to attend the same PDL. How do you know who should attend a given PDL session? Consider everyone's role, experience, and capacity for buy-in. It is entirely appropriate to start small and build your audience in subsequent work from your earliest adopters.

One year, we hosted a series of math clinics in my region. The clinics were a great idea—in theory. However, our initial planning was based on the assumption that these clinics would be relevant to all districts and all elementary grades. Unfortunately, our interpretation of the data analysis we had done wasn't entirely correct, and in the end, we had to cut back on our offerings and even cancel one of the workshops because enrollment numbers were too low. By jumping to conclusions without sufficient information, we ended up under-delivering on our intended purpose. The learning we took away from this? Never assume that a good idea for PDL will translate into something that is "sure-fire." All PDL requires thoughtful and appropriate planning.

Act: Make it a Team Effort

Professional development planning should never be an individual responsibility. Like other creative endeavors, it requires multiple minds to make the best decisions. Who should be involved with the development of professional learning? You'll likely want to include the building or district leader responsible for overseeing the work involved, the PDL facilitator, and—most important—a number of people the PDL is intended to help.

To reach out to these stakeholders, use the initial data you've collected as a starting point, which makes it much easier to solicit the people you need. Even though time and other responsibilities are always at the forefront of everyone's mind, an opportunity to shape PDL that will make a difference is one that few are willing to miss. An added benefit of having all of these stakeholders involved in the planning is that it circumvents the "Whose idea was this session, anyway?" problem. When you or someone else can respond with "It was an idea we all felt was important," it reminds everyone that they are in it together.

When we were looking to design an effective math curriculum project PLC that would be applicable to our entire region, my office had to weigh the interests of a number of districts. By querying our region for program usage and then engaging in a few targeted outreach phone calls and in-person meetings, we were able to run a program that both had the support of the region and was large enough to be effective. We could not have done this without looking at data and planning alongside districts in our community.

Act: Think Strategically About Format

Even after PDL planners clarify a solid purpose and rationale and get all the right players together, they can still be stymied from developing a truly tremendous PDL session if the form that it takes doesn't fit the function that the rationale speaks to. Consider the following example. About five years into my teaching career, my principal had an excellent idea. Teachers wanted to engage in learning about topics of their own choosing with others (akin to the work of professional learning communities, or PLCs, even before the term became popular). My principal, therefore, wanted to give teachers time to fit this into their schedules, but she wasn't sure how. Ultimately, she decided to use faculty meeting time at the end of the day and felt that combining the necessary administrative information with group PLC time would be a great way to give people what they wanted in the time that was available. Unfortunately, the end of the day—when people are often tired—was a tough time for people to think creatively, and it was often challenging to fit the PLC work we needed into faculty meeting time. When the year was done, many who were initially excited about the PLC work had lost much of their enthusiasm.

This principal began with the right steps. She thought carefully about the purpose of the work, and she used audience voice to craft the sessions (as teachers were able to consider exploring topics of their own choosing), but she had not given the sessions the form that best fit the purpose. This example speaks to the importance of form fitting function when it comes to PDL. She learned that focused sessions at a time of day when people felt energized could have made this PDL more effective.

So, how do we make sure that a particular form and function fit well together? The best way is to put ourselves in the shoes of those doing the work. Here are some questions to consider when determining a format that aligns to the purpose of your particular PDL session:

- What will make the experience most conducive to learning for those in the room? Should the facilitator work with the whole group, in small groups, or both?

- When should the work take place? Does everyone need to engage in the work at the same time?
- What location should be used for the work? What facilities need to be available? How will the site be prepped for this work? What technology is required, and how should it be set up? How will the furniture in the room be arranged? Will materials be put out for participants the night before? That morning? Some other time?
- What feedback should be collected, and when should that be done? How should it be gathered?
- As the planner, when should you be present? When shouldn't you?
- If I were going to be attending the PDL session being planned, what would help me learn best? What expectations would I have? Never forget the necessity of having empathy.

There isn't one right answer to any of these questions, but what's important is that we ask them. If we can provide clear answers to these questions, then we can rest assured knowing that form and function will fit. If we can't marry the two, then we have two choices: either we reconsider the PDL design or we rethink our true purpose.

Act: Consider Logistics

Our main focus should be on the purpose, players, and format, but we also have to give serious consideration to how the event will play out. This means that all PDL, if done well, should cover the following:

- Contracts and negotiations
- Partnerships
- Length of school day
- Time of year

Contracts and negotiations are beyond the scope of this book, but they are worth mentioning. If you hope to engage in deep professional learning, you need to take all of the necessary measures to set the stage for that learning to happen. Negotiating for professional learning should never be an adversarial experience. After all, with the success of learners as the end goal, who wouldn't agree with the importance of PDL? Nevertheless, negotiating and contracting for PDL time does require answering some tough questions. For example, the more time you request, the more others may ask where that time will come from. There is only a finite amount of time in a given year. One of the worst ways to deflate professional development possibilities is to assume that more learning tasks can be piled on people's shoulders in the same space and time.

Partnerships are also important to consider. Fully internal PDL has the advantage of allowing you to build an experience from the ground up and cultivate leaders in your chosen topic. In some cases, such as when you have a purely district-based initiative, this makes sense. However, partnerships outside the realm of a school or district can also be incredibly powerful. Let's look at two different ways to craft partnerships.

Internal and External Communication. Tapping the knowledge of external experts to assist staff in ways that cannot be done internally is an excellent way to help form meet function and ensure that the purpose of your PDL can be realized. How do you access external experts? Having an established network of educators is incredibly helpful. In my region, we operate a listserv for assistant superintendents and directors of curriculum, which is used as a clearinghouse for identifying consultants and thought leaders who excel at providing professional development in a variety of areas. If your region doesn't have something like this, social media can be an excellent resource. For instance, in assisting our region with PDL planning, I've helped make connections between colleagues and educators I met through Twitter. We share great ideas about various topics in this network, from curriculum design to national policy. Recently, I utilized my network to collect information about making science fairs more about science and less about the fair. I was also able to put an assistant superintendent in my region in touch with two educators with specific expertise in this area.

District-to-District Support. Another interesting partnership opportunity is when districts partner with each other to provide PD on a larger scale. This does not happen as much as it should; districts are regularly insulated and naturally concerned with their own local challenges. However, if we forever remain in our district silos, we miss an excellent opportunity to expand our learning further than we would have otherwise. Chances are, if your district finds an initiative important, then there are others nearby who feel the same way. For example, we recently designed a collaborative professional development service program, where districts exploring an initiative of their own can open up sessions to their neighbors in an effort both to foster cross-district collaboration around a given initiative (e.g., academic vocabulary, Response to Intervention, or engaging in difficult conversations) and to share costs for consultant expertise. Imagine what educators can learn about themselves—and one another—when professional development goes beyond school and district boundaries and focuses on the needs of an entire community.

Planning for professional development without considering logistics misses a tremendous opportunity to see the process as more than just individual trees. We have to always keep the forest in mind as well. Take length of school day, for instance. When are you most creative? What about your colleagues? How often are you asked this question when professional development is designed in your school or district? Though I tend to do my best thinking in the morning, I respect the fact that this might not be the case for everyone. Therefore, it is important to make sure that you build variety into the time of day during which learning sessions are designed. This requires forethought and a willingness to step outside of the scheduling box.

In addition, time of year is also important to consider. The beginning and end of the year are notoriously difficult times to get any educator, whether learner or leader, to engage in exploring new opportunities. It isn't that these are "impossible" times to begin PDL initiatives, but we must understand that the beginning of the year is typically fraught with many unknowns, and the end of the year is dominated by summative, wrap-up tasks. It is understandable that our brains may simply be too full at these times. Providing a few weeks to settle in before exploring sizable PDL initiatives allows for staff and students to be sufficiently rested—both physically and emotionally—so they can engage in new and innovative work.

Review: Put It All Together

Once you've planned your PDL efforts, it's important to reflect on the process. Remember that reflection isn't something you only do at the absolute end of an experience. In fact, it is more powerful when you continually reflect throughout. So, after coming up with a plan, it is crucial that you and your team consider a number of key questions:

- Was I able to marry form and function to give this design what I believe will be a lasting impact? Why or why not? (If you weren't able to marry these two, consider spending more time thinking about the purpose and rationale. Even better, share the purpose and rationale with a colleague. Does he or she clearly see the connection?)

- Are there any minor last-minute adjustments I can make before the PDL begins to achieve a better fit? (If there isn't enough time to ask yourself these questions, then you aren't providing enough lead time in your preparation. Sometimes we do our best work when we have the chance to step back, see the big picture, and make necessary changes.)

- Did I involve the right players? How do I know? Who was under- or over-represented? (Take a moment to consider the purpose of your professional learning again. Will it meet the needs of the audience you intend it to? Remember, you can't answer that question by yourself; you need the input of the audience itself to truly know.)

- Was the purpose and rationale well designed? Why or why not? (The best way to know this before the PDL experience is to consider how intuitive the connection is between your agreed-upon goal and the process. You can't answer this question entirely alone, either. Ask a colleague and a participant to help you judge.)

- What logistical factors weren't explored enough? What factors were explored too much? (Nobody's perfect, but logistical mistakes have a way of becoming easily visible. If planning steps such as scheduling and sending follow-up emails aren't your forte, then make sure you have someone on your team who excels at keeping the details in check.)

This is also a great time to consider where you stand with respect to your assessment and feedback strategies. A main goal of any PDL feedback is to gauge whether you've met your purpose and where attendees see the next steps taking them. The best methods of gathering feedback are those that provide data you can use; ask thoughtful, poignant questions; and aren't particularly long or involved (assuming this feedback will be supplied at the end of a learning session, when participants are likely tired from a full day of learning). Therefore, a question such as "Was this an effective

PDL session for you?" wouldn't be the best choice because it doesn't generate a lot of deep thinking or provide you with actionable feedback. By contrast, a question such as "What two changes to this PDL would you recommend that might result in an even greater effect on your practice?" is a much better option because it encourages participants to think and provides you with targeted responses.

You can never plan too much, which makes Phase I so important. As Ben Franklin so aptly reminded us at the beginning of this phase, when we don't give planning its due, we're likely due for a headache. It pays to plan early and often and to make sure we devote enough time to this phase before moving on to the next. Once you begin the providing phase, there is no turning back!

PDL Phase II: Providing

"The great aim of education isn't knowledge, but rather, action."

—Herbert Spencer

Our work as educators is only as good as the action we take. Despite the physical and mental exertion that goes into providing PDL, this phase doesn't have to become all-encompassing if we've planned well and made time to reflect and follow up. In fact, if you'll allow me, I'd make the case that this phase of the PDL process is like the center of an Oreo cookie. If we protect the center with structurally sound bookends (i.e., planning and following up), then we're apt to discover an incredibly rich and substantive central phase. The analogy may be a stretch, I know, but I think you get the point.

Before you bite into that PDL cookie, let's explore how the TAR method plays out in this phase. Consider the following questions for individual reflection:

Think: How can I use what I know about my learning space and the participants' unique backgrounds and needs to adapt the PDL appropriately?

Act: What implementation steps should I take when facilitating (or leading the facilitation of) PDL?

Review: In what ways can I reflect during the process of providing PDL so I can course correct "on the fly"?

Think: Assess the Lay of the Land

There are many corollaries between teaching young students and working with adult learners. Just as we would expect classroom teachers to know about their students prior to engaging in instruction, we should expect PDL facilitators to know their audience prior to engaging with them. The facilitator should have gained a fair amount of in-depth knowledge during the planning phase, but now is the chance to gain additional insight. Here are some key issues to consider as you begin the session:

- If your session offered open enrollment, this might be your first time seeing a full roster of participants. What are their backgrounds? What are their current roles? Are they attending the PDL session with colleagues in the same role or from the same building?
- This may also be your first opportunity to explore your space. How will you set it up? How will you make it comfortable and a conducive environment for learning?
- Powerful PDL requires you to be prepared down to the smallest details, but it also requires you to be flexible based on the needs of the learners with whom you'll be working. Remember that flexibility never equals a lack of preparation. In fact, more flexibility is often a sign of better preparation. After all, if we have a good command of our role in the PDL process, then it makes it easier for us to meet others where they are.
- What are some quick and easy strategies you can use to build relationships from the start?
- Is everyone engaged? How can you course correct during implementation and change your facilitation strategies to ensure that you're meeting the needs of all attendees?
- How can you facilitate PDL while also letting your participants take the reins?

Think: Establish Meaningful Relationships

Engaging in conversation with attendees as they arrive and during breaks is critical to the success of your learning session. Chatting with educators throughout the day as they process their thoughts will provide valuable insight you can use to inform your own thinking as the PDL session progresses. You'll also get a sense of some of the ways in which people learn best, where trouble spots in your facilitation could be, and how much structure you'll need to build into the schedule, such as discussion time or break time. Adapting the session to best fit their needs helps keep the learning relevant and engaging, which will ensure that their experience has a lasting impact. Even as you talk with participants throughout the learning session, you may notice that some of these items change and shift.

Recently, I was involved in a training session that was tied to New York state performance assessment measures, and I realized that many of the participants were curious about the state's new science standards and were wondering if New York would be moving toward the Next Generation Science Standards or if the standards would be something entirely different. Even though the topic of the training wasn't truly tied to these standards, I found that it was imperative to make a course correction for two reasons. First, I knew that the only way to keep participants' interest was to tie our training to the questions they were asking. Second, I knew that fear and anxiety can derail even the most engaging learning sessions. The questions that were being posed weren't necessarily fearful ones, but if I was remiss in answering them, the participants could become consumed by them. I realized it was necessary for me to take this "teachable moment" and change course so we could eventually reach our final destination.

Act: Make It Happen

Powerful PDL doesn't happen on its own. The best facilitators have spent countless hours developing their practice to make learning meaningful. I could never hope to explore all of their keys to success in this book, but here are three that can't be ignored.

Keep the *A*s in your *agenda*, but don't be afraid to modify the parts in the middle. Time is your best friend and your worst enemy during a PDL session. Participants who arrive early expect you to start on time, and everyone present expects the session to end as scheduled. Make sure you hold to these, but don't be afraid to make changes along the way to meet learners where they are. When I build an agenda, I always make sure that I have a hard start and hard stop that I won't deviate from, but I often build much more flexibility into the middle part of the session and have a few different pathways I can follow. I've found this allows me to spend more or less time on a specific agenda item without compromising the session itself.

Laugh, learn, and lead. Facilitators who are people first, are willing to take a backseat when necessary, and stand on their experience are those who are most effective because they relate to their audience, help everyone let their guard down, and build up attendees' experience by sharing their own. I can't begin to tell you the number of times these three *L*s have guided me as a facilitator. I rely on humor constantly because I find that nothing gets past the jitters of meeting new learners for the first time like well-placed humor. Another key for me? Letting my attendees pick up on some of the facilitation. Everyone attending a session deserves the opportunity to serve as a leader for a while. It should never be me (or any other single person) 100 percent of the time.

Prepare to hear others as much as you expect to be heard. If you're going to reflect and follow up on the session effectively, you have to be physically and mentally present. Being an active listener when facilitating is key to a successful session. You might have expertise, but you're never an expert. Listening to what people need and acknowledging their successes and struggles will help you navigate your facilitation work. Remember that you'll never run out of information to share, but you can run the risk of never learning exactly what information your audience truly needs if you don't make it a point to be present and listen.

Act: Be a Participant

Much can be learned from being a participant in the professional learning you have either designed or are facilitating. However, it isn't common for those who have designed the PDL to stay for more than a few minutes if they aren't the ones facilitating. This is a challenge for a couple of reasons.

- If you don't play an active role in providing PDL, then you can't tell whether the facilitator is, in fact, on target with the goals and vision for the work. That means you can't provide feedback and you won't really be able to move in an appropriate direction for those you serve. This tends to take the stickiness out of the PDL.

- If you don't spend more than a moment invested in the PDL, then you can't get a sense from the participants of how well the session resonates with them, what their continued needs are, and how to help meet those needs.

During your time as a participant, you should be interacting with other participants and asking questions tied to the learning at hand, the process, and the logistics. You should also engage in the activities you're present for, if for no other reason than to get a feel for what the participants are experiencing, minute by minute. This is also a great time to take pictures and video you can later share with your community (and beyond). Too infrequently are PDL sessions made visible beyond those in attendance. If we want to build better professional development, we have to help the wider world of education see what it looks like. Don't forget that being a participant should be something we all look forward to—because it's fun!

A note for facilitators: It's important to find time to be a participant in your own session too. This means you might have to give the floor to attendees for an extended period of time so you can measure how individuals, small groups, and the whole group is progressing. These so-called "room temperature checks" at various points are helpful, but we can learn so much more if these checks feel less like a pause in instruction and more like you're turning over the floor. If the structure of your work doesn't allow you to sit in on your own session, then make sure you have someone in the audience who can serve as an impartial critic—someone who can provide you with the feedback you need during the session. Remember that feedback is always better in the moment, as the session is happening, rather than at the end when it's too late to course correct.

Review: Right the Ship as you Navigate

Another reason to be an active participant in your own PDL is that it makes it easier to steer the PDL while it is being provided. Facilitators want their sessions to be effective, and having an observer on hand makes it much easier for session leaders to make adjustments as needed. As a participant, you can share insight from what you've seen and conversations you've had and help make sure that as the session progresses, it becomes even more meaningful. Some of the best feedback a PDL facilitator or designer can receive is that the second half of the work was more engaging and relevant than the first. When you hear this, all signs point to successful course corrections and an understanding that facilitation, like all good education, is never one size fits all.

During a recent professional development session for teachers, I noticed that a group of attendees seemed less engaged than the rest. They were chatting and sharing vacation photos on their phones. During a break, I had a nice conversation with the facilitator about what I had noticed and what could be done to help bring those participants into the fold. I asked the facilitator to share what she was seeing; after all, this wasn't only about my interpretation of events. She mentioned she was aware of their conversations and hadn't addressed them because she had worked with these educators previously, before becoming a consultant. We talked about why this might prove to be a distraction for others in the course who weren't aware of their prior relationships. After the break, the consultant facilitated some changes and held this group of educators more accountable for paying attention, and she seemed to more effectively be able to draw them in to the larger discussion.

Review: Collect, Constantly

Your facilitation is never simply about output. Instead, you're collecting input every second you're serving as a facilitator. The data you collect will help you not only during facilitation but also as you transition into the next phase of designing sticky PDL. What sort of data are you hoping to collect? Certainly, qualitative data will be readily accessible from participants' statements as they enter the session, from their discussions during the session, and from their feedback responses after the session. This is another reason why a facilitator needs to be present during all aspects of PDL.

Quantitative data can also be easily gathered from participants. Using any number of digital devices and feedback apps, it's possible to quickly assess where participants are in their learning. You don't even have to go digital! A simple measure such as "Fist to Five" (where participants show, by the number of fingers they hold up, their comfort with a topic or idea) can go a long way to collecting data that can be quantified. Data collection during the providing phase provides you with an opportunity that end-of-session data does not: it allows you to change your facilitation moves to match where your participants are—one of the most important moves any leader of learning can make. If possible, you can also enlist the help of an observer who can collect data while you facilitate. Although this isn't always possible, when it is, it provides you with the opportunity to be fully focused on your facilitation while your peer is collecting and crunching the numbers.

Remember the quote from Herbert Spencer at the start of this phase? If not, here it is again: "The great aim of education isn't knowledge, but rather, action." Spencer was right. Even though planning and follow-through really serve as the foundation to our PDL, we live and die (figuratively speaking, of course) by providing. Since all stakeholders see every detail of this phase (as opposed to the few who see the planning and following-up phases), our effectiveness at providing has the biggest influence on how learners and leaders grow in their professional development.

So what's the takeaway? The key idea to providing successful PDL is to make sure that you truly know your audience, learn as much as you lead, and be flexible in your facilitation. Your attendees are not simply clones of you. If we can think of these characteristics as the mantra for the providing phase of PDL, then we'll likely be able to get from one side of our Oreo cookie to the other without losing the filling.

PDL Phase III: Following Up

"We have to follow up if we ever expect any follow through."
—Anonymous

In *The Mirage*, a recent research report from The New Teacher Project (2015), we learn that despite the roughly $18,000 districts spend on teacher improvement per educator each year (in some cases, it's close to 10 percent of a district's entire budget), only 30 percent of teachers see measurable improvement in practice. And even though close to 50 percent of the educators surveyed feel that professional development is tailored to them, "every development strategy, no matter how intensive, seems to be the equivalent of a coin flip: Some teachers will get better, and about the same number won't" (p. 22).

When it comes to professional development for learning, it seems as if you're damned if you do, and you're damned if you don't. As educators, though, we know that isn't an acceptable answer. If we choose not to give up on student learning, then we must make the same choice for adult learning.

The Mirage focuses on three primary ways to do this: redefine, reevaluate, and reinvent the PDL that we design. To truly change how we all experience professional development, we have to think deeply about what has already taken place and make practical changes to our actions for the future. Let's look at how the following-up phase and its integral steps can make a difference on your PDL.

As we embark on this third phase, consider the following questions for individual reflection:

Think: How can I use data collected during the providing phase to come up with ideas for change?

Act: In what ways can I use these collected data to help facilitators (and myself) improve practice?

Review: How do I use my work in this phase as a springboard toward putting new PDL into action?

When we follow up on what we've done, it is a great opportunity to use the information we've gained from previous phases to inform our work in the future. Hopefully, through the first two phases, you've gained worthwhile data that can help you continue to improve the PDL experience for those you serve.

Be sure that anyone providing PDL understands that this phase is just as important as the first two. Data can't be ignored or forgotten. Otherwise, how will you be able to supply the facilitator with the information needed to get better? Make time for evaluation to be a mandatory part of every PDL session; ask leaders of learning to build it into their work at all costs!

Think: Analyze, Don't Scrutinize

Now that you've got your data from your PDL session, it's time to start your analysis. This means you'll want to take a look at all the information you've received from participants, marry it to the data you collected during the learning session itself, and start combining it into information that is valuable not only to you but also to whomever facilitated the learning session. Look at the data from a number of different angles. For instance, does the collected data confirm your interpretation of how the session went as you were either facilitating or participating and watching the facilitation? What surprises do the data share? Can you gather corroborating evidence through conversations with participants or by looking at attendees' work? Be comfortable asking "What ifs?" For example, "What would the data show if we designed this learning session to last two days instead of one?" or "What if this learning series existed in a co-facilitated format?"

It's also important to consider why attendees responded to the evaluation the way that they did. Use your rosters to determine where attendees came from and what background knowledge and biases they may have brought to the session. Assuming you had the chance to play the role of an observer (or facilitator), consider how what you saw agrees or disagrees with attendees' comments. Look to see if the various roles and job titles of participants resulted in different learning for everyone. Then summarize your findings, share them with your facilitator, and save a copy for your records. We forget how things truly went after we're a bit removed; keeping these summaries handy makes sure that you don't experience the same mistake twice (or three times).

Sometimes we have to make decisions about whether we're going to run professional learning sessions multiple times. All too often, a number of months go by before we decide to put it together again. By keeping written summaries of feedback, it becomes much easier to refresh your memory about the success of a particular session. As an example, when it came time to decide whether to host a series of mindset and mindfulness workshops, I was fortunate enough to have the feedback on hand from the last time we ran the workshop. With overwhelmingly positive evaluations, we not only decided to hold the sessions again but also designed a new session tying together mindset and formative assessment. Professional development for learning should always be designed with data in mind.

Act: Recognize the Importance of Good Team Communication

How do you share feedback that's great? How do you share feedback that isn't so great? It's important that your learning facilitators hear honest and specific feedback, and it's important that you be the one to share it with them. Sharing positive feedback can be as easy as an email summary or a phone call to debrief. Sharing the more difficult feedback is never easy, but it helps to keep the following in mind.

- **Remember that it's never about you or the other person.** It's about outcomes and occurrences, so keep the conversation about the *what* and not the *who*. Consider what attendees shared and why it matters, and ask for feedback from the facilitator. If the provider's opinion differs from the attendees', ask what needs to be done to make sure everyone sees things the same way. If there is agreement, consider what should be done to get better results moving forward. As Stone, Patton, and Heen (2010) discuss in *Difficult Conversations,* "Your invitation [to problem solve] is more likely to be accepted if you offer the other person an appealing role in managing the problem" (p. 156). It is important to work together to address any necessary changes, rather than to work apart.

- **Set goals.** How do you use what didn't work to make sure that it will next time? Talk about how you will support the facilitator in achieving collaborative, reachable goals, and remember that in some cases, you have the flexibility to choose not to work with someone again in the future.
- **Tie it back to why.** If we focus on why we're doing things, then it becomes easier to get past hang-ups regarding the how or what. If we are in agreement on the fact that we're providing PDL to help others better their practice, then it becomes much easier to move the conversation forward. Don't be afraid to constantly refer back to the why, as the "why of things" tends to influence how sticky PDL can become.

Act: Check In

In addition to communicating with your facilitator, you should be reaching out to attendees. What did they find most valuable in the session? What was least valuable? A survey might put out the welcome mat, but you actually have to open the door to invite people in. This means reaching out to past participants to see what the feedback they provided actually means. Along with contacting them in reference to specific inquiries, you're also networking with your learners. Most feedback instruments serve a tremendous purpose in data collection, but they often feel very impersonal. But an email or a phone call? That's all about the connections. Part of the stickiness factor to PDL is humanizing it; we need to make sure that participants feel connected at the start, during the learning, and after it's done as they continue on their journey.

There's also other information that can be queried through a check-in. Who requested additional PDL opportunities you already have planned and can share? Who can you tap to assist with future PDL development? Who shared some amazing insights that you can use in promotional work? One of the greatest aspects of working on professional learning design is when you can connect a recent participant to upcoming offerings tied to their growth path. These nudges may not result in anything tangible, or they may turn into tremendous opportunities for those you serve. You'll never know until you reach out. This is also an opportunity to connect attendees to one another. A series of PDL offerings we are now offering were precisely because a number of educators at separate sessions had been asking for workshops that were designed around the maker movement. By connecting learners and leaders to each other, we were able to design a series of basic training sessions, as well as a facilitators group for those educators leading maker initiatives in their schools and districts.

Take any opportunity to follow up! Whenever a connection can be made, we should be making it. For example, I make it a point to reach out whenever I see feedback that warrants it. While chatting with educators face to face is always preferred, even a quick email can make a huge difference. And remember that attendees' interests don't go cold quickly after a session, so if you can't reach out immediately, don't write it off as a lost opportunity. Professional learning is built on the premise of continuous improvement, and this continued communication is critical to help outline the path for learners to keep moving forward.

A really great aspect of the work I do is helping teachers expand their practice by providing them with opportunities to serve as teacher leaders. After a recent math chairperson's meeting, I struck up a conversation with one of the math chairs. She mentioned loving the math offerings we were providing but feeling as if we weren't representing statistical concepts as deeply as we needed to be in the era of the Common Core State Standards. She pitched an idea for two workshops right there on the spot. After a number of conversations and some back and forth around planning, we decided to host both of her workshops, and they both had excellent attendance.

We should never hesitate to reach out to the learners who are the direct beneficiaries of this work, regardless of whether they are children or adults. Are they seeing changes in their classrooms? Has learning become more engaging for them over the last week/month/year? What would they like to see their teachers do more of? Remember that learning is never about one session; reaching out is an opportunity to make sure that you've done all you can to make sure everyone sees learning as a continuing endeavor.

Review: Go Back to Get to the Future

The following-up phase is just as much about "next time" as it is about "last time." Once you've analyzed your data, studied your findings, and connected with attendees to keep their learning relevant, it's time to create a feedback loop that will take you from "now" to "then." It's important to remember that reflection is more than just a thinking process. When we review, we have to be willing to use any knowledge gained to make changes the next time we're involved in PDL design. Otherwise, we're apt to mimic Sisyphus, continually pushing that rock up the hill with no change, no progress, and—clearly—no real learning taking place.

During the spring, as we start to consider PDL offerings for the next year, we constantly refer back to our previous offerings. What was well received? What wasn't? Why? We also ask ourselves what initiatives are evergreen and which are more "flavor of the month." How can we support a district's desire to explore both ends of that spectrum? Archiving emails and evaluation summaries is incredibly helpful here. Like a well-staged movie or play, we're apt to perform best when we feel like we're really there.

So, here we are, at the conclusion, and also back to the beginning of our PDL process. The best PDL is cyclical, and each experience we design should be connected to work done in the past. Like the repetitive nature of the TAR method itself, keeping a circular nature to professional development for learning design helps keep our learning sticky and helps us remain invested in the work and our growth from it.

Research, both new and old, reveals much about professional development that needs to change. But if we remember that PDL represents different things to different people and that if we take the time to put thought, action, and review into our planning, providing, and following up, then we can underline the L in PDL and make the experience something that truly leads to meaningful learning.

Acknowledgments

Like true professional development for learning, writing a book only works when many more people than the author (or PDL planner) alone are involved. With that in mind, I have to express my gratitude to the following people for helping me think, act, and review over the last two years as this book has taken shape. Genny Ostertag, Susan Hills, and Jamie Greene helped me turn a series of loose ideas into a tightly woven guide. Walter McKenzie reminded me that we should never move on until it is actually time to do so. My ASCD L2L PLC (how's that for a bunch of acronyms) always helped me remember to ask for assistance and encouraged me to keep my guard down, something that any writer needs to live by. Marla Gardner and the team at Putnam Northern Westchester BOCES provided me with the support necessary to truly think deeply about professional development for learning, supported my work on this book, and taught me much of what I know. My family has supported my writing and my work in the profession, and they kept me honest by always asking, "How's the book coming?" My wife, Laurie, has been by my side for the last 18 years, and during the writing of this book, that has not changed. She always reminds me of what is most important. Finally, to Sydney and Ardyn, who are just two of the reasons why we must always make sure that professional development sticks.

To give your feedback on this publication and
be entered into a drawing for a free ASCD
Arias e-book, please visit
www.ascd.org/ariasfeedback

ENCORE

"DOS AND DON'TS" FOR CREATING STICKY PROFESSIONAL DEVELOPMENT

Phase	TAR Step	Don't	Do
Planning	Think	Don't plan PDL as a "flavor of the month."	Take your time. PDL planning is rarely done quickly. Your purpose should always be the guiding principle to help you cut through the noise about the hottest PD trends and to make good decisions about what works best for your team.
	Act	Don't plan PDL without those who will serve as participants.	Think of your audience. If the PDL is meant to benefit teachers, then your teaching team must be involved in the planning. Since the true goal of PDL is to eventually benefit students, consider having young learners involved in PDL planning as well.

Phase	TAR Step	Don't	Do
Planning	Review	Don't start thinking about data at implementation; it leaves the facilitator at a severe disadvantage.	Plan out the data you collect and how you plan to use it even before implementation begins. This includes deciding on qualitative and quantitative measures, as well as how you'll eventually evaluate the data later on.
	Think	Don't treat everyone in the audience as if they are at the session for the same reason.	Treat your audience as the individual learners they are. Gather as much data as you can about them prior to facilitation, and do your homework on your facility ahead of time to accommodate the needs of each learner.

Phase	TAR Step	Don't	Do
Providing	Act	Don't simply facilitate a PDL session without also assuming the role of participant.	Remember that serving as a participant during the learning is the best way to collect data and help your audience make meaning. Whether you're providing the PDL or you're there to observe those who are, remember to use your participant status to collect data, get to know your audience, and take the "motivation temperature" of those learning from the session.
	Review	Don't get so married to the agenda that you can't make course corrections when needed.	Understand that aside from keeping to a start time and an end time, an agenda is just a document. You need to constantly think about your implementation as it proceeds, and you need to be ready to change course if the situation requires it.

Phase	TAR Step	Don't	Do
Providing	Think	Don't underestimate the value of thoughtfully harnessing data.	So many of us treat data collection like a boring chore; we do it for the sake of collecting without realizing its potential to inform and transform PDL. Your implementation is only as good as the phases that surround it. This means that in order to build great PDL facilitation, you have to ask key questions. In order to do that, you have to truly analyze the data you collect to help you plan. This means that multiple stakeholder groups should be considering the data, tying it all to the initial purpose, and making targeted decisions about what to do with the results. No data should get left behind.

Phase	TAR Step	Don't	Do
Following Up	Act	Don't assume that facilitators have learned all they need to know from the providing phase itself.	You wouldn't expect a teacher to pick up everything that happens in his or her classroom while teaching, and the same is true for facilitators. Even experts need feedback. Feedback should always be focused, constructive, and done in person or via a phone call. (Use email only for confirmations and positive follow up.)
	Review	Don't forget to connect the dots between PDL events.	Even when PDL opportunities cover vastly different topics, the data and feedback from a PDL session should serve as an introduction to planning future sessions. When you see PDL as a web or network, in which each session is connected to and informs subsequent sessions, you'll never lose sight of the common goal: deeper learning for educators and a better education for our students.

References

Basye, D. (2014). Personalized vs. differentiated vs. individualized learning. ISTE. Retrieved from https://www.iste.org/explore/articleDetail?articleid=124

Gallup, Inc. (2014). Understanding perspectives on American public education: Results of a Gallup-*Education Week* survey of K–12 school district superintendents—Survey 2. Retrieved from http://www.gallup.com/services/178973/understanding-perspectives-american-public-education-survey.aspx

Gladwell, M. (2000). *The tipping point.* New York: Little, Brown.

Guskey, T. (2009). What works in professional development? *Phi Delta Kappan.* Retrieved from http://www.k12.wa.us/Compensation/pub-docs/Guskey2009whatworks.pdf

Guskey, T. (2014). Planning professional learning. *Educational Leadership, 71*(8), 10–16.

Kaestle, C. et al. (2001). *School: The story of American public education.* Boston: Beacon Press.

Stone, D., Patton, B., & Heen, S. (2010). *Difficult conversations: How to discuss what matters most.* New York: Penguin Books.

Teacher Development Trust. (2015). *Developing great teaching: Lessons from the international reviews into effective professional development.* London, UK: Author. Retrieved from http://tdtrust.org/about/dgt

The New Teacher Project. (2015). *The mirage: Confronting the hard truth about our quest for teacher development.* Brooklyn, NY: Author. Retrieved from http://tntp.org/assets/documents/TNTP-Mirage_2015.pdf

About the Author

Fred Ende is the assistant director of curriculum and instructional services for Putnam Northern Westchester BOCES, one of New York's 37 regional education service agencies. In this role, Fred assists districts in the metropolitan New York City area with curriculum and professional development, design, and evaluation, and he also serves as a regional liaison with the state education department. Prior to his work at BOCES, Fred taught middle school science and served as a department chair for 10 years in Chappaqua, a suburb of New York City. Fred is an ASCD Emerging Leader and currently serves as New York ASCD's vice president. Fred is passionate about designing professional development that leads to deep learning and believes in the importance of collaboration across school, district, and regional lines to design learning opportunities that are truly sticky. Fred can be reached at fende@pnwboces.org and on Twitter at @fredende.

Related ASCD Resources

At the time of publication, the following ASCD resources were available (ASCD stock numbers appear in parentheses). For up-to-date information about ASCD resources, go to www.ascd.org. You can search the complete archives of Educational Leadership at http://www.ascd.org/el.

Print Products

17,000 Classroom Visits Can't Be Wrong: Strategies That Engage Students, Promote Active Learning, and Boost Achievement by John Antonetti and James R. Garver (#115010)

Balanced Leadership for Powerful Learning: Tools for Achieving Success in Your School by Bryan Goodwin, Greg Cameron, and Heather Hein (#112025)

Building Teachers' Capacity for Success: A Collaborative Approach for Coaches and School Leaders by Pete Hall and Alisa Simeral (#109002)

The Highly Effective Teacher: 7 Classroom-Tested Practices That Foster Student Success by Jeff Marshall (#SF117001)

Igniting Teacher Leadership: How do I empower my teachers to lead and learn? by William Sterrett (#SF116039)

Insights Into Action: Successful School Leaders Share What Works by William Sterrett (#112009)

School Leadership That Works: From Research to Results by Robert J. Marzano, Timothy Waters, & Brian A. McNulty (#105125)

Teacher Teamwork: How do we make it work? by Margaret Searle and Marilyn Swartz (#SF115045)

THE WHOLE CHILD The Whole Child Initiative helps schools and communities create learning environments that allow students to be healthy, safe, engaged, supported, and challenged. Professional Development That Sticks relates to the supported and challenged tenets. To learn more about other books and resources that relate to the whole child, visit www.wholechildeducation.org.

For more information: send e-mail to member@ascd.org; call 1-800-933-2723 or 703-578-9600, press 2; send a fax to 703-575-5400; or write to Information Services, ASCD, 1703 N. Beauregard St., Alexandria, VA 22311-1714 USA.

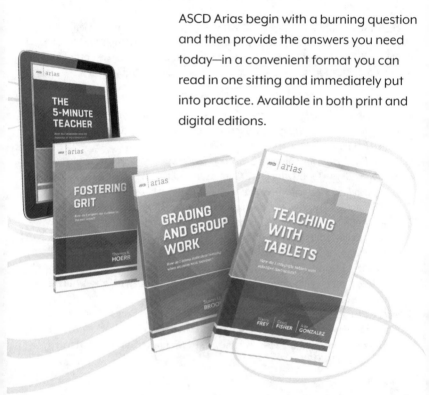